GREAT CAREERS WORKING WITH
ANIMALS

by Derek Moon

FOCUS
READERS.
NAVIGATOR

WWW.FOCUSREADERS.COM

Focus Readers is distributed by North Star Editions:
sales@northstareditions.com | 888-417-0195

Produced for Focus Readers by Red Line Editorial.

Photographs ©: Shutterstock Images, cover, 1, 4–5, 7, 8–9, 11, 13, 14–15, 17, 19, 20–21, 25, 26–27; Abigail Waldrop/Fort Bliss Public Affairs/DVIDS, 23; Red Line Editorial, 29

Library of Congress Cataloging-in-Publication Data
Names: Moon, Derek, author.
Title: Great careers working with animals / by Derek Moon.
Description: Lake Elmo, MN : Focus Readers, [2022] | Series: Great careers | Includes index. |
    Audience: Grades 4-6
Identifiers: LCCN 2021011859 (print) | LCCN 2021011860 (ebook) | ISBN 9781644938515
    (hardcover) | ISBN 9781644938973 (paperback) | ISBN 9781644939437 (ebook) | ISBN
    9781644939857 (pdf)
Subjects: LCSH: Animal specialists--Vocational guidance--Juvenile literature. | Veterinary
    medicine--Vocational guidance--Juvenile literature. | Zoologists--Vocational guidance--
    Juvenile literature. | Zoology--Research--Vocational guidance--Juvenile literature.
Classification: LCC SF80 .M66 2022 (print) | LCC SF80 (ebook) | DDC 636.0023--dc23
LC record available at https://lccn.loc.gov/2021011859
LC ebook record available at https://lccn.loc.gov/2021011860

Printed in the United States of America
Mankato, MN
082021

ABOUT THE AUTHOR

Derek Moon is an author and avid Stratego player who lives in Watertown, Massachusetts, with his wife and daughter.

TABLE OF CONTENTS

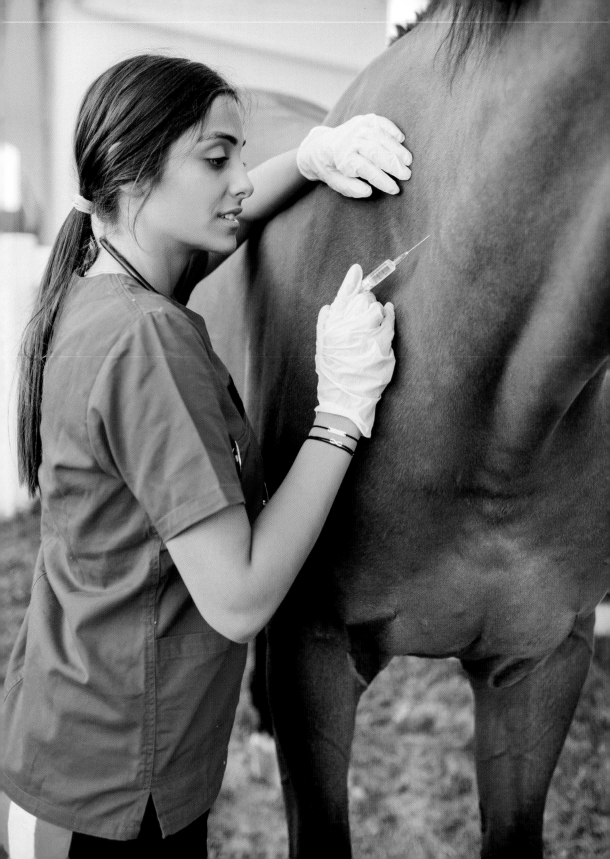

CHAPTER 1

ANIMALS ARE AWESOME

When people think about careers working with animals, they often picture veterinarians. In particular, they think of vets who care for pets. But in reality, vets work with many different kinds of animals. Some vets treat farm animals. Other vets work at zoos. Vets may even treat animals in the wild.

Livestock veterinarians work with large animals such as cows, horses, and pigs.

In addition, vets are just one of the many careers that involve animals. Some people study animals and their **habitats**. In many cases, these jobs involve working outdoors. People must go out where the animals live.

Other jobs focus on training or caring for animals. For these careers, working

SCIENCE STUDIES

Working with animals often requires understanding science. Many colleges have degrees for specific jobs. For example, students might major in zoology or wildlife conservation. Other students may choose a more general course of study. Biology is especially important for many animal careers. Chemistry, ecology, and forestry can also be helpful.

Dog walkers may work with several animals at one time.

with animals is not the only part of the job. Interacting with other people can be just as important.

There are dozens of careers that involve animals. But they all have one thing in common. They require a love of animals.

CHAPTER 2

ANIMAL MEDICINE

Animal medicine involves keeping animals healthy. There are several careers in this field. Veterinarians are doctors who treat animals. Many vets work in clinics. They perform checkups on animals. They also create treatment plans for animals that are sick or injured. They perform **surgeries**, too.

Dogs are the most common animal treated at veterinary clinics.

Vets often specialize in certain kinds of animals or treatments. For example, some vets work with exotic animals. Other vets work with livestock. They help farmers manage large groups of animals. Some vets work in labs. They study diseases and try to find cures. Their work helps other vets treat animals.

WILDLIFE REHABILITATION

Sometimes wild animals get sick or injured. In other cases, a baby animal may become separated from its mother. These animals often need special care to return safely to the wild. Wildlife **rehabilitators** help make a safe return possible. They work with vets to create plans. They help each animal regain the strength or skills it needs to return to the wild.

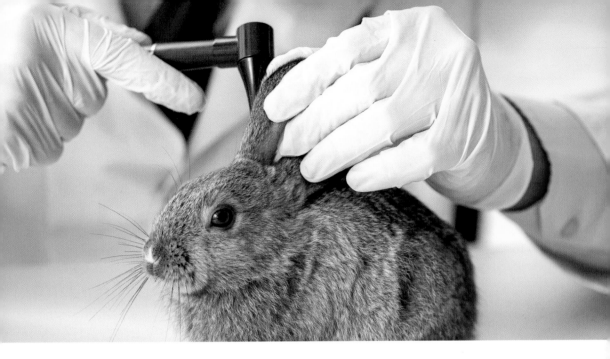

A technician may perform tasks such as examining an animal's ears.

Technicians and assistants also play important roles in animal medicine. Technicians are similar to nurses. They help vets treat animals. For example, technicians might take blood or give shots. Assistants support vets by doing basic tasks. They might feed animals or do office work.

WILDLIFE VETERINARIANS

Many veterinarians work in offices. But there are outdoor options, too. Wildlife vets are trained to work with wild animals. For this reason, they are often out in nature.

Wildlife vets perform a wide variety of tasks. For instance, they provide routine care to animals in the wild. They respond to emergencies. And sometimes they perform advanced procedures such as surgeries.

The daily life of a wildlife vet depends on where he or she lives. For example, a wildlife vet in northern Canada might take a helicopter deep into the wilderness. She may spend one day checking on a herd of caribou. On another day, she may treat an ailing eagle. And sometimes she

Wildlife vets may help birds that have injured wings.

may run a clinic in town. Becoming a wildlife vet can be a great choice for people who enjoy variety and adventure.

CHAPTER 3

STUDYING AND PROTECTING ANIMALS

Our planet is home to millions of animal species. Many careers involve studying, protecting, and caring for these animals. Zoologists and wildlife biologists are scientists who study animals. Some work in labs. However, many work outdoors. They visit the animals' habitats. Zoologists typically

Marine biologists may dive underwater to study life in the ocean.

focus on understanding the animal itself. They often specialize in certain types of animals. For example, ornithologists study birds. Ichthyologists study fish. In contrast, wildlife biologists focus more on the relationships between animals and their habitats.

Scientists do research to learn about animals. For instance, they might observe animals' behaviors or diets. They might also look into how humans' actions are affecting animals.

Some scientists track the population of animals in an area. If the population goes up or down, they try to understand why. Scientists often conduct experiments,

A scientist who studies apes may go deep into the jungle to observe them.

too. Then they write reports about what they learned.

Other jobs focus on protecting animals. Some scientists work with government officials. They create rules and plans that protect animals and their habitats. Other scientists work at wildlife preserves or nature centers. These areas offer safe places for animals to live. Some scientists help rare animals have babies. That way, the animals will not die out.

Conservation officers make sure people follow the rules relating to wild animals. They patrol outdoor areas such as parks or nature preserves. They also make sure people have **licenses** to fish or hunt. Conservation officers might also lead educational courses. For instance, they may explain how humans' actions are harming certain animals.

Zookeepers manage animals that live in zoos. Aquarists manage animals that live in aquariums. Both of these jobs

One of a zookeeper's many jobs is to educate visitors.

go far beyond just feeding the animals. Zookeepers and aquarists make sure the animals stay clean and healthy. They also make sure animals get enough exercise. In addition, they help clean and repair the spaces where the animals live. Their work helps the animals stay healthy and safe.

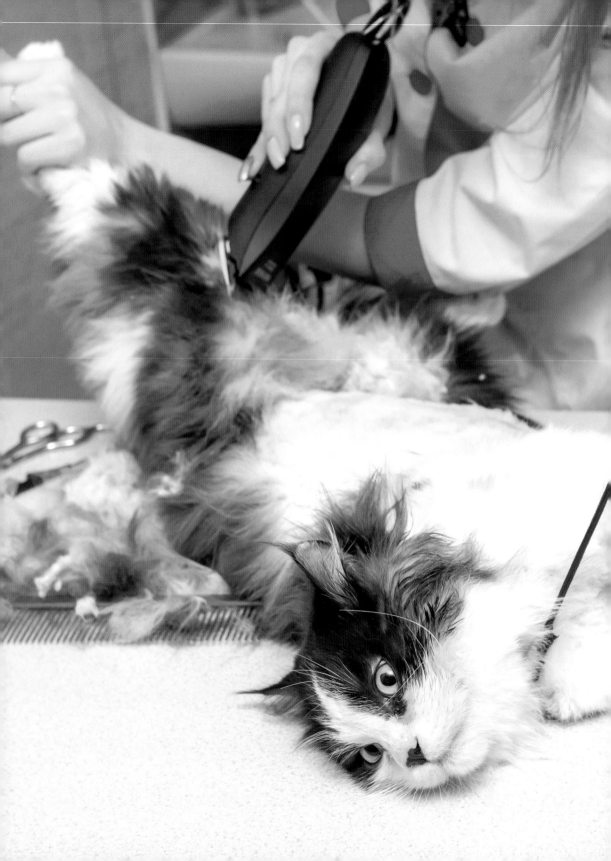

CHAPTER 4

CARING FOR ANIMALS

Humans have close relationships with many animals. They ride horses. They raise animals on farms. And they keep many other animals as pets. As a result, there are many careers related to caring for these animals.

A wide variety of jobs involve caring for pets. For instance, groomers keep pets

Groomers offer services such as haircuts and nail trims.

21

looking good. Kennel workers take care of animals while their owners are away. And dog walkers make sure people's four-legged friends get enough exercise.

Many jobs involve training animals. Obedience trainers help people teach their pets tricks and commands. Some animals are trained to have advanced

BREEDING ANIMALS

Breeders mate animals and then sell the babies. Good breeders study **genetics**. They plan how to help the animals be healthy and strong. Breeders also help people choose a pet that will be a good fit. They match the needs of the people with the needs of the pet.

Military dogs are trained to perform specific tasks, such as finding bombs.

skills. For example, some dogs help farmers herd cows or sheep. Other dogs help soldiers and police officers. In addition, service dogs help people with disabilities. A trainer teaches specific skills to the dog. When the animal is ready, the trainer continues working with the dog's new owner.

Some trainers work with animals in **captivity**. For instance, marine animal trainers care for animals such as whales and dolphins. These trainers make sure the animals have enough food, exercise, and mental activity.

Other trainers get animals ready for competitions. For example, horse trainers prepare horses for races and shows. Dog handlers travel with their dogs to competitions. The dogs might do a sport such as agility.

Some people take classes to learn these jobs. But **apprenticeships** can be even more helpful. Apprenticeships help people learn while working.

POLICE DOGS

Some police officers get help from specially trained dogs. Police dogs have a variety of skills.

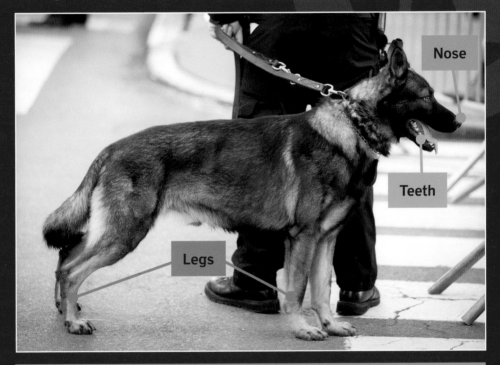

Nose

Teeth

Legs

Nose: Dogs have a much stronger sense of smell than humans do. Police dogs can be trained to find hidden weapons, drugs, and other illegal materials.

Legs: Police sometimes need to cover a lot of ground in a short amount of time. Police dogs can chase down a suspect.

Teeth: Police dogs may use their teeth to hold a suspect who is threatening the safety of others.

CHAPTER 5

ENTERING THE FIELD

Each career with animals requires a different set of skills. Some jobs require a science background. With others, a person can learn everything on the job. The best-paying jobs often require advanced education. For example, veterinarians start by getting a four-year college degree. Then they have four more

Science classes are often helpful for people who want careers working with animals.

years of vet school. Finally, they must get a license.

Zoologists and wildlife biologists typically need a college degree, too. In some cases, an advanced degree is also required.

Not all animal jobs require a college education. For instance, no degree is needed to become a veterinary assistant. Pet grooming and obedience training do not require a college degree either. Instead, workers learn on the job. They may also get a **certificate**.

Working with animals isn't easy. Many jobs require long hours or working on weekends. The work can be physical, too.

For example, workers might have to lift or maneuver heavy animals. But for people who love animals, the hard parts are worth it. Working with animals can be a fun and rewarding career.

CAREER PREP CHECKLIST

Interested in a career with animals? As you move into middle school and high school, try these steps.

1 Look for ways to learn more about animals. Reading articles is a great place to start. Visiting the zoo can also help you build a stronger understanding of animals.

2 Study hard in school. Science subjects such as biology and chemistry are especially important. But subjects such as math and business can be important, too.

3 Talk to a guidance counselor about your interest in animals. This person can help you learn about specific careers that fit your interests.

4 Look for local clubs or organizations for people with similar interests.

5 Some zoos and animal shelters accept volunteers. Volunteering can be a great opportunity to see what it would be like to work in that setting.

6 Find a professional in the career you're interested in. Ask if you can shadow that person for a day and learn about what he or she does.

FOCUS ON
GREAT CAREERS
WORKING WITH ANIMALS

Write your answers on a separate piece of paper.

1. Write a paragraph explaining the main ideas of Chapter 4.

2. Do you think it would be more interesting to work with pets or wild animals? Why?

3. What type of education does a wildlife biologist need?

    A. certificate
    B. college education
    C. apprenticeship

4. Which career might involve helping an injured gorilla in the jungle?

    A. zoologist
    B. conservation officer
    C. wildlife veterinarian

Answer key on page 32.

GLOSSARY

apprenticeships
Positions where young people learn a trade and receive low wages in return for their work.

captivity
When an animal is under the control of humans, often in a zoo or aquarium.

certificate
A document that shows a person has completed a certain type of training.

genetics
A type of science relating to traits and molecules inherited from parents.

habitats
The types of places where plants or animals normally grow or live.

licenses
Formal or legal permission to do something.

rehabilitators
People who help restore movement and other abilities after an injury.

surgeries
Medical procedures to fix problems inside the body.

TO LEARN MORE

BOOKS

Bedell, J. M. *So, You Want to Work with Animals?: Discover Fantastic Ways to Work with Animals, from Veterinary Science to Aquatic Biology.* New York: Aladdin, 2017.

Swanson, Jennifer. *Absolute Expert: Dolphins.* Washington, DC: National Geographic, 2018.

Wild, Gabby. *Wild Vet Adventures.* Washington, DC: National Geographic Kids, 2020.

NOTE TO EDUCATORS

Visit **www.focusreaders.com** to find lesson plans, activities, links, and other resources related to this title.

INDEX